COUNTRY Jam Trax

FOR GUITAR

Interior design and layout by Don Giller
Cover and package design by Inkwell, Inc.
Audio cassette duplication by Core Systems, Inc.
Packaging manufactured by Wedgewood Associates, Inc.

Copyright © 1992 by Amsco Publications,
A Division of Music Sales Corporation, New York, NY.

All rights reserved. No part of this book may be
reproduced in any form or by any electronic or mechanical means
including information storage and retrieval systems,
without permission in writing from the publisher.

Order No. AM 87432
US International Standard Book Number: 0.8256.1324.8
UK International Standard Book Number: 0.7119.2859.2

Exclusive Distributors:
Music Sales Corporation
225 Park Avenue South, New York, New York 10003 USA
Music Sales Limited
8/9 Frith Street, London W1V 5TZ England
Music Sales Pty. Limited
120 Rothschild Street, Rosebery, Sydney, NSW 2018, Australia

Printed in the United States of America by
Vicks Lithograph and Printing Corporation

Amsco Publications
New York/London/Sydney

Table of Contents

Introduction	3
Country Sea	4
The Country Gentleman	7
Daydreamin'	9
Rockabilly Truth	11
Three-Quarter Ballad	14
Triple Trouble	17
Country Rock	19
Light Fingerpickin' Blues	21
A Cajun Dance	24
The Tricky Ricky Rag	27
The Upbeat Cowboy	30

Introduction

Country music has long enjoyed one of the largest markets in the music industry. Today, with cable television offering several channels that feature both live country music performances and country music videos, more and more people are being exposed to what is truly a diverse and increasingly popular American art form.

Hi, I'm Ralph Agresta, and once again I'd like you to join me and my musician friends John Abbey (bass), Phil Cimino (drums), and Phil Ricciardi (keyboards) for a country music jam where we play the rhythm-section parts and you play the solos.

The eleven tracks featured on the tape and in this book present a varied sample that includes many of the different styles, tempos, chord progressions, and keys that are commonly found in country music.

As anyone who is familiar with the JamTrax series already knows, these tapes and books can be enjoyed by musicians at any level. More experienced players can use the tape to experiment with new soloing ideas and techniques or for warming up before gigs. Beginners can experiment with the scales and patterns provided for each tune and practice soloing with a live band without the pressure that often comes from playing in front of other people.

As you listen to the *Country JamTrax* tape, you will notice—along with the obvious exclusion of any electric or acoustic lead guitar parts—that many of the instruments that are traditionally used to add color to country music (pedal steel guitar, Dobro, fiddle, mandolin, harmonica, and accordion—to name a few) have also been consciously omitted. This was done in an attempt to allow enough musical space so that you and any number of your musical friends can simultaneously jam along and trade solos over the basic tracks.

In the pages that follow, along with the suggested scale patterns and riffs, you'll find complete chord charts for each tune that will guide you through the structure of each jam.

Good luck, have fun, and, as always, I sincerely hope that you enjoy and learn from this book and tape.

Country Sea

Try these major pentatonic scale patterns in C, F, and G.

Pattern 1: C major pentatonic scale

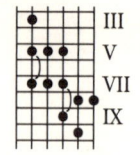

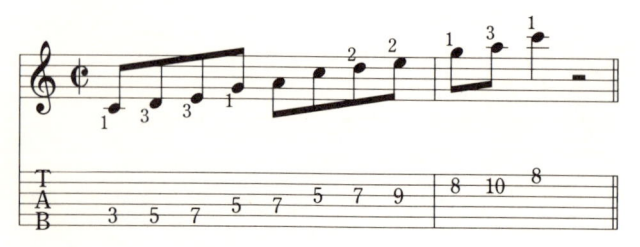

Pattern 2: F major pentatonic scale

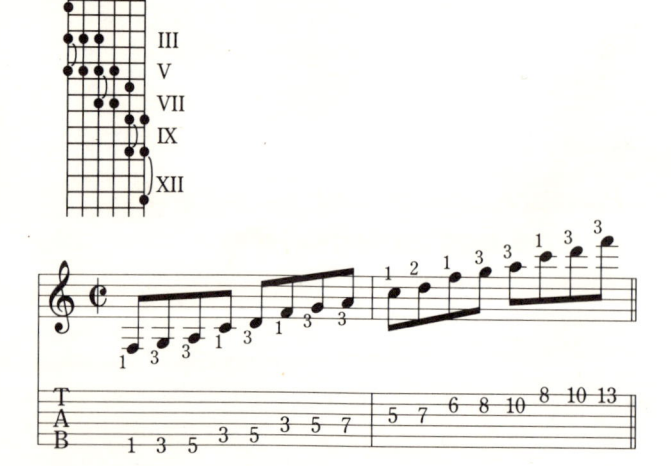

Pattern 3: G major pentatonic scale

Notice that this pattern is the same as Pattern 2 transposed up one whole-step (two frets).

Pattern 4: Major arpeggio riff in C, F, and G

This pattern features a minor third note which is often used in a major-chord arpeggio as a passing tone to approach the major third note. This riff will work over a C chord when played in seventh position, over an F chord when slid down to first position, and over a G chord when played in third position.

Pattern 5: C major scale with pickup and extension

Pattern 6: D7 riff

Here is a variation on the riffs from Pattern 4 that you can use to play over the D7 chord in measure 11. Notice that it leads smoothly into the G chord in measure 12

To play over the F Minor chord in measure 14, use Pattern 2 but make sure to avoid the major third note (A).

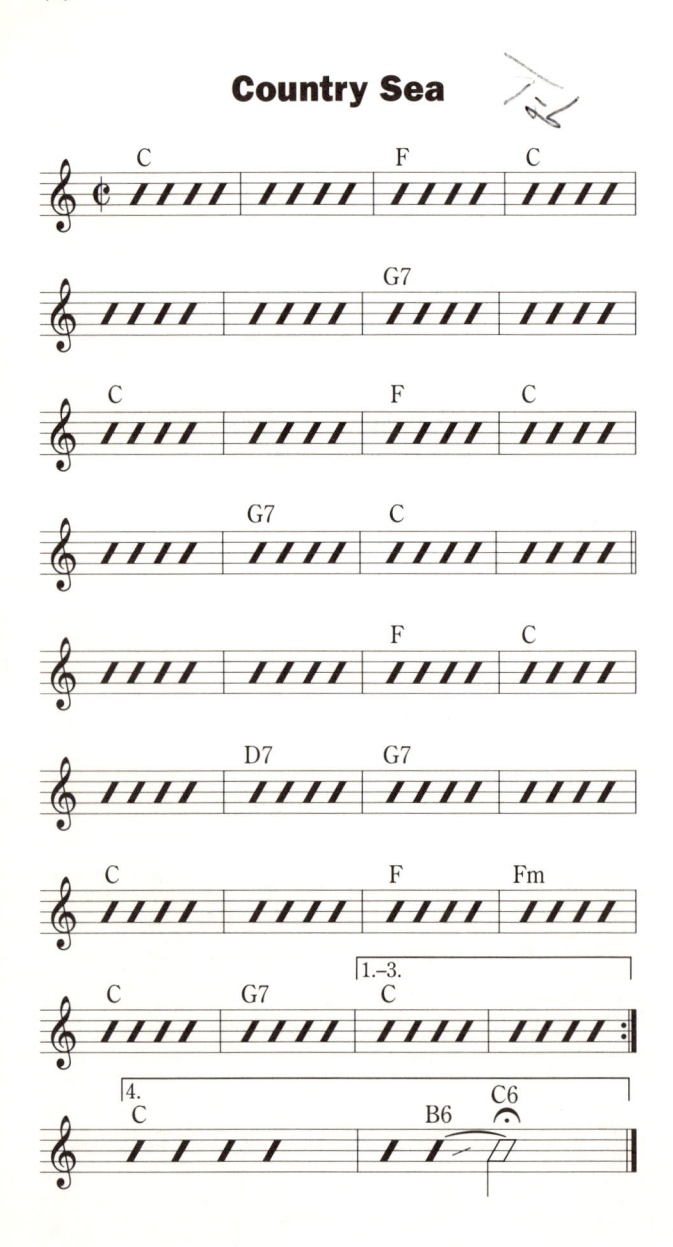

Country Sea

The Country Gentleman

Pattern 1: D major scale with D major pentatonic pickup

This pattern starts out as a D major pentatonic scale, but the second measure is a one-octave D major scale.

Pattern 2: D major scale (one-octave)

Pattern 3: D major scale (two-octave)

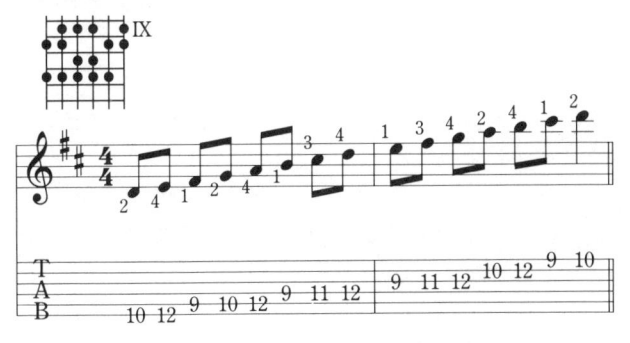

Pattern 4: G major pentatonic scale with open strings

7

Pattern 5: A7 slide riff

This is the type of fluid riff that works well in a medium-tempo country song like "The Country Gentleman." You could also use an A major pentatonic scale over the A7 chords:

Pattern 6: G# diminished arpeggio

The Country Gentleman

Medium shuffle

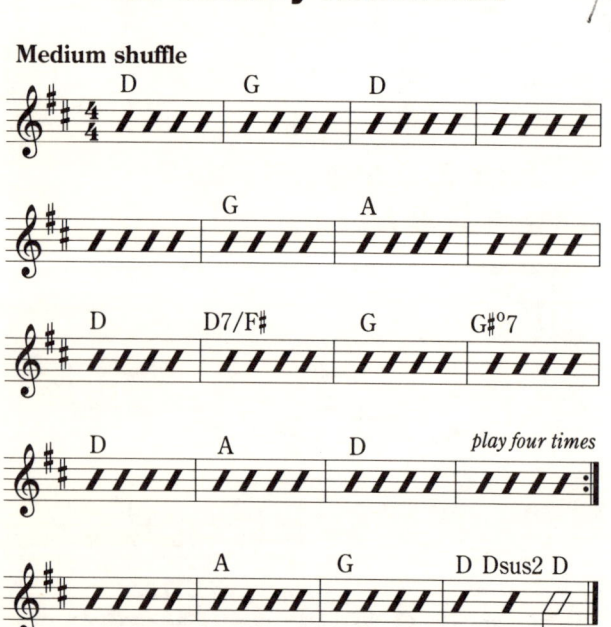

D	G	D	(D)
G	A	(A)	(A)
D	D7/F#	G	G#°7
D	A	D	*play four times*
(D)	A	G	D Dsus2 D

Daydreamin'

Pattern 1: F major scale (two octave)

Pattern 2: B♭ major scale with pentatonic pickup

The first measure of this pattern is a B♭ major pentatonic scale, which leads into a one-octave B♭ major scale.

Pattern 3: C Mixolydian scale with extension

A *Mixolydian* scale is a major scale with a flatted seventh note. Try this one over the C7 chords.

Pattern 4: G minor scale (two-octave)

Pattern 5: F major scale in thirds with pickup

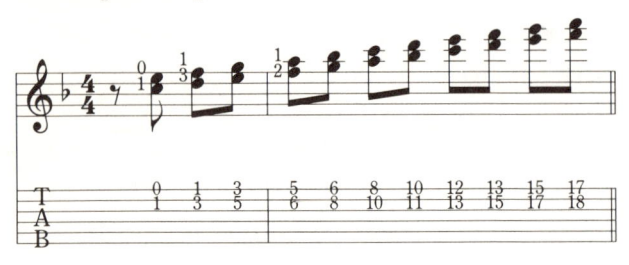

Pattern 6: F major scale in sixths

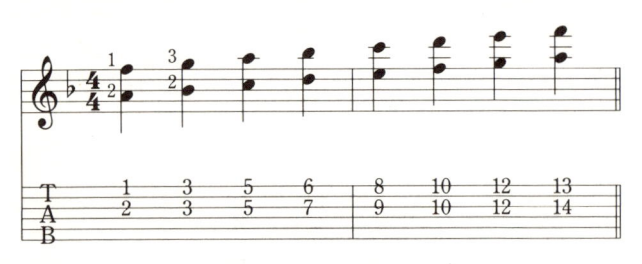

Daydreamin'

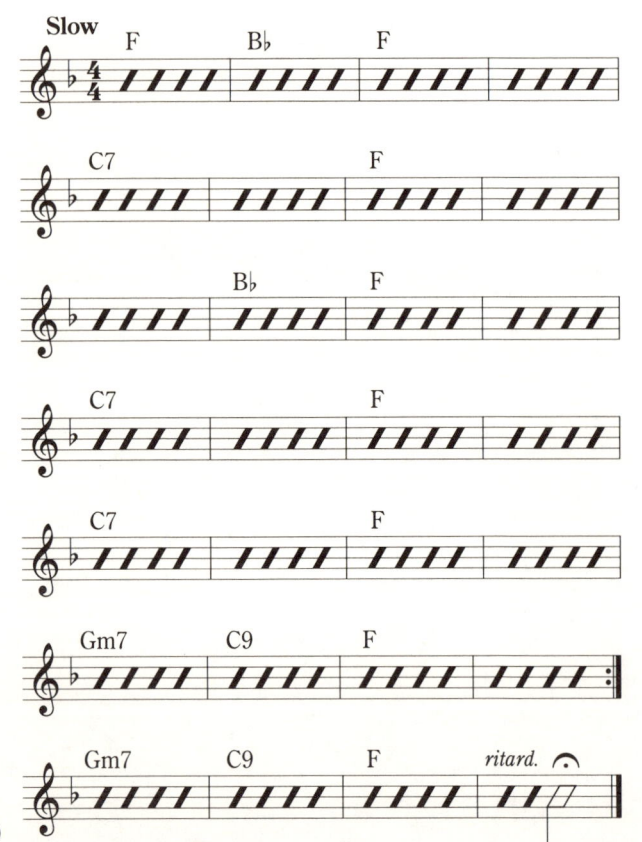

10

Rockabilly Truth

Try these major pentatonic scale patterns in E, A, and B. Notice that these patterns substitute the minor third for the more usual major second. Remember that the minor third is often used as a passing tone to approach the major third.

Pattern 1: E major pentatonic with minor third (no second)

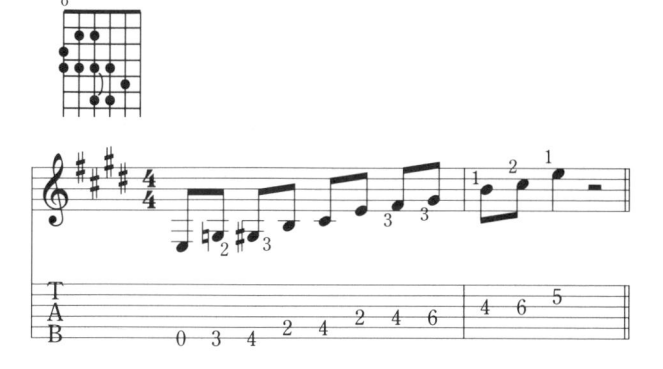

Pattern 2: A major pentatonic with minor third (no second)

Pattern 3: B major pentatonic with minor third (no second)

Pattern 4: E minor pentatonic

Pattern 5: E minor pentatonic pulloff riff

This riff is based on the E minor pentatonic pattern above but with the addition of several notes taken from the E major scale and the flatted fifth (B♭).

Pattern 6: E Mixolydian riff

The descending line in this riff goes right down the E Mixolydian scale (with the addition of a hammeron from minor to major third at the end).

Pattern 7: E diminished/chromatic riff

This riff makes use of chromatic notes and notes from an E diminished arpeggio. Try using it to move from the A chord to the E.

Rockabilly Truth

Medium shuffle

Three-Quarter Ballad

Country musicians often refer to $\frac{3}{4}$ time as *waltz time* or *three-quarter time*. This "Three-Quarter Ballad" contains the kind of typical changes that you will find in songs like The "Tennessee Waltz" or "Take It to the Limit."

Pattern 1: C major scale (open-position)

Pattern 2: F major scale (two-octave)

Pattern 3: G Mixolydian scale (two-octave)

Remember that a Mixolydian scale is simply a major scale with a flatted seventh. This makes the Mixolydian a good choice for soloing over the V chord; in this case, G.

14

Pattern 4: C major scale in sixths with extension

Patterns 5 and 6: Arpeggio riffs

These two riffs feature slides and arpeggios on most of the major and minor chords found in "Three-Quarter Ballad."

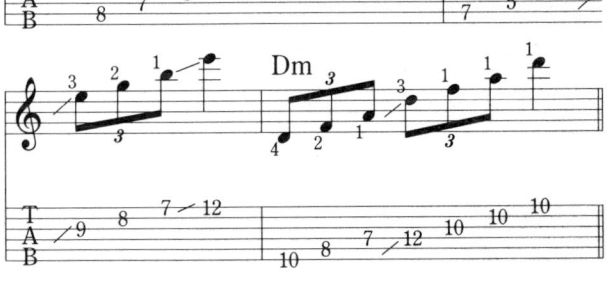

pattern 5

let ring ----| *let ring* ---| *let ring* ---|

pattern 6

Three-Quarter Ballad

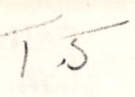

Moderately slow waltz

Triple Trouble

In "Triple Trouble" you will get a chance to use all of your scales and riffs in the key of G. Here are a few more riffs that will give you some soloing ideas for this tune.

Pattern 1: First-position slide/ hammeron riff

Use this type of riff over measures 5 through 8, 21 through 24, or 37 through 40.

Pattern 2: Chromatic double-stop riff

This one works well over measures 45 through 48.

Pattern 3: G7 arpeggio

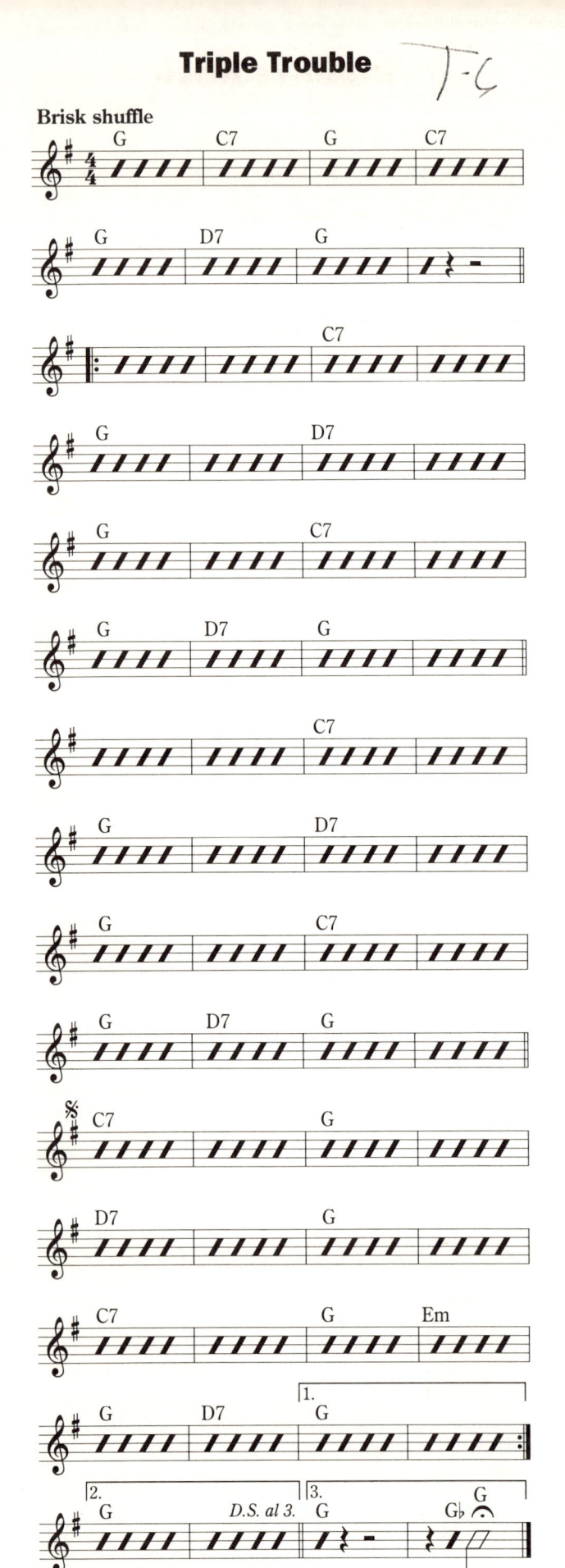

Triple Trouble

Country Rock

Pattern 1: A major pentatonic scale (three-octave)

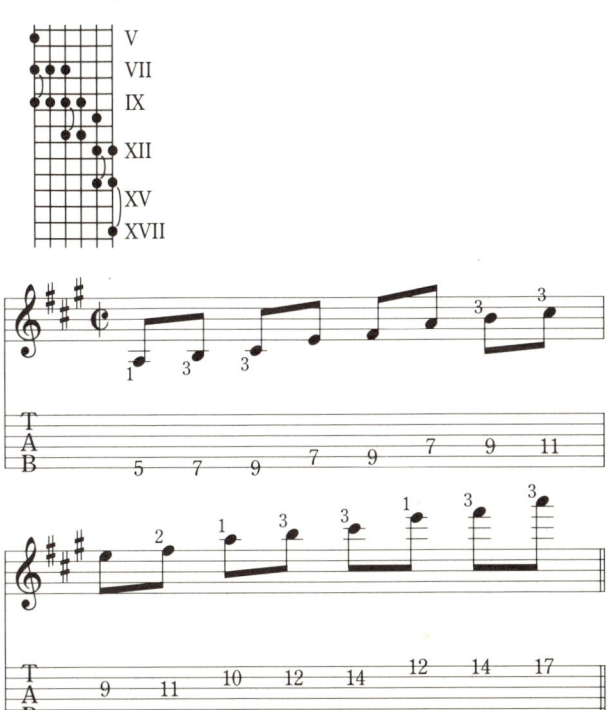

Pattern 2: A Mixolydian scale (two-octave)

Pattern 3: First-position A major pentatonic scale (two-octave)

Pattern 3: First-position A major pentatonic riff

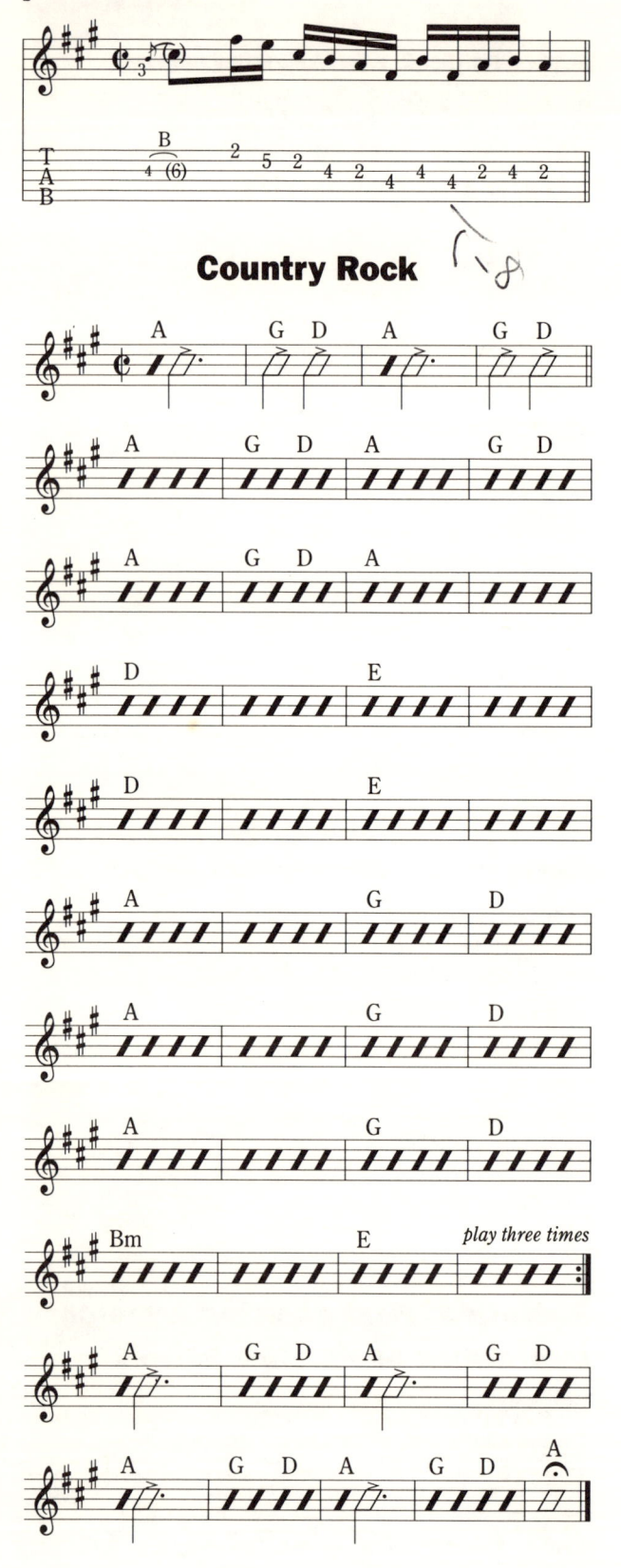

Country Rock

Light Fingerpickin' Blues

This track is a good one to use for practicing your bottleneck, or slide, playing.

Pattern 1: B7 slide riff

This type of pattern gives a bluesy touch to the B chords in the progression. This riff leads nicely to the A because the pattern contains all of the notes of an A chord. Try some variations using the notes in the accompanying diagram.

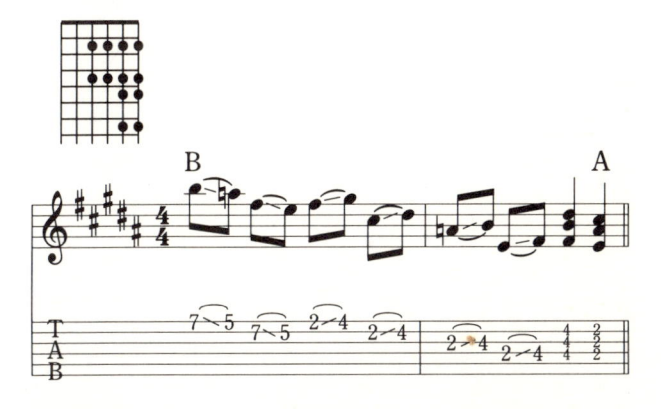

Patterns 2, 3, and 4: E7, F#, and A riffs

The following riffs are based on the same box pattern used in Pattern 1 shifted to E, F#, and A.

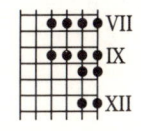

pattern 2

pattern 3

pattern 4

Pattern 5: B blues scale

Obviously, you can also play "straight" guitar over this track. This B blues scale fits in nicely.

Pattern 6: F# blues scale with passing tones

This is basically a transposed version of the pattern above but with the addition of a few passing tones taken from an F# major scale. Be careful not to dwell too much on the A notes; these minor thirds should be used to lead up to the major third, A#.

Light Fingerpickin' Blues

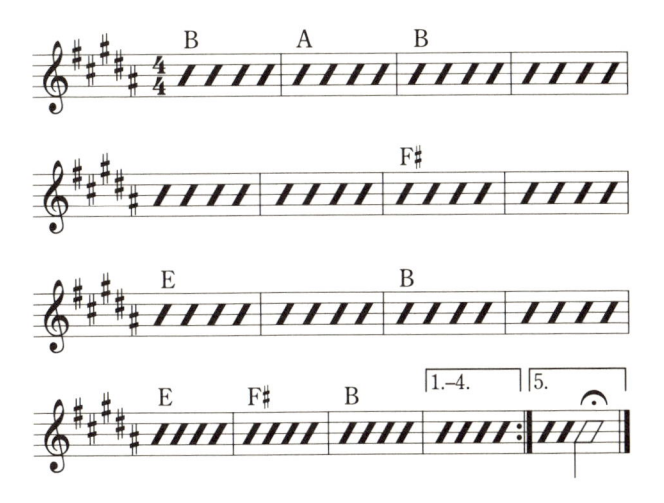

A Cajun Dance

Pattern 1: D pentatonic scale with minor third (two-octave)

For "A Cajun Dance," add this D major pentatonic pattern to the similar ones in E, A, and B from "Rockabilly Truth." Notice that the flatted-third passing tone replaces the second in the lower octave.

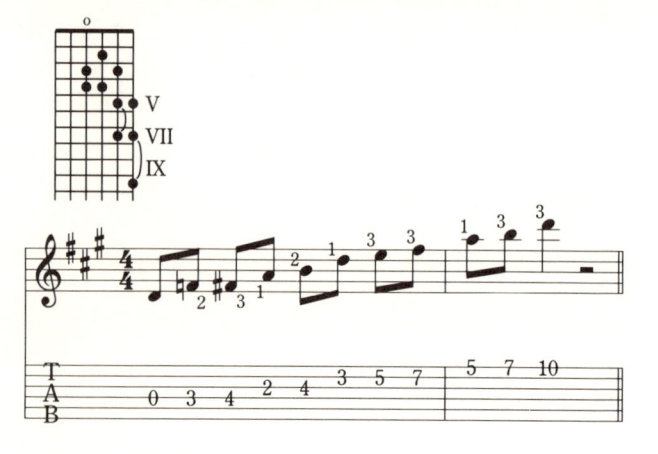

Pattern 2: D Mixolydian scale

Pattern 3: D pentatonic/Mixolydian riff

This riff combines elements of the two patterns above. Notice the slight differences in fingering that make the riff easier to play.

let ring - - ┤

Pattern 4: Chromatic double stops

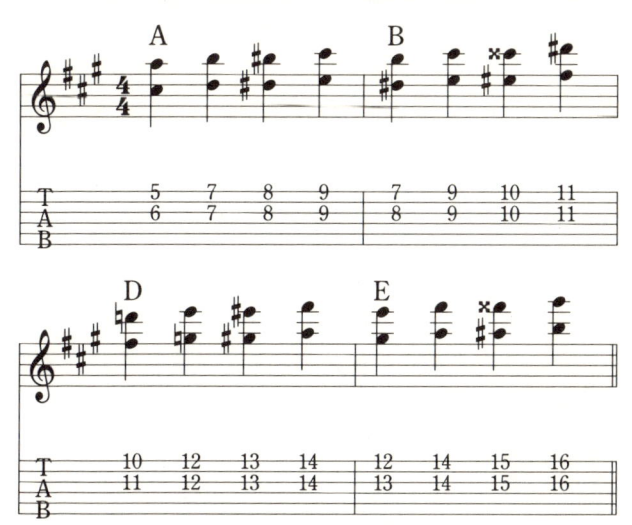

Pattern 5: Chromatic A-to-D riff

This is a good riff to use in measure 4 to kick off your solo—or use it in measure 12, 29, or 37 to lead smoothly from A to D.

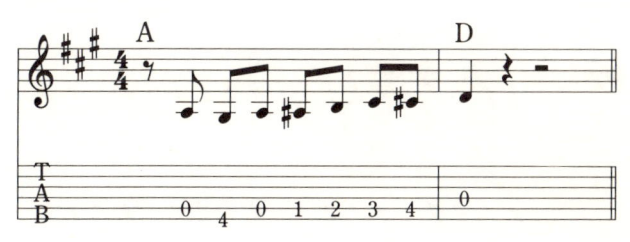

A Cajun Dance

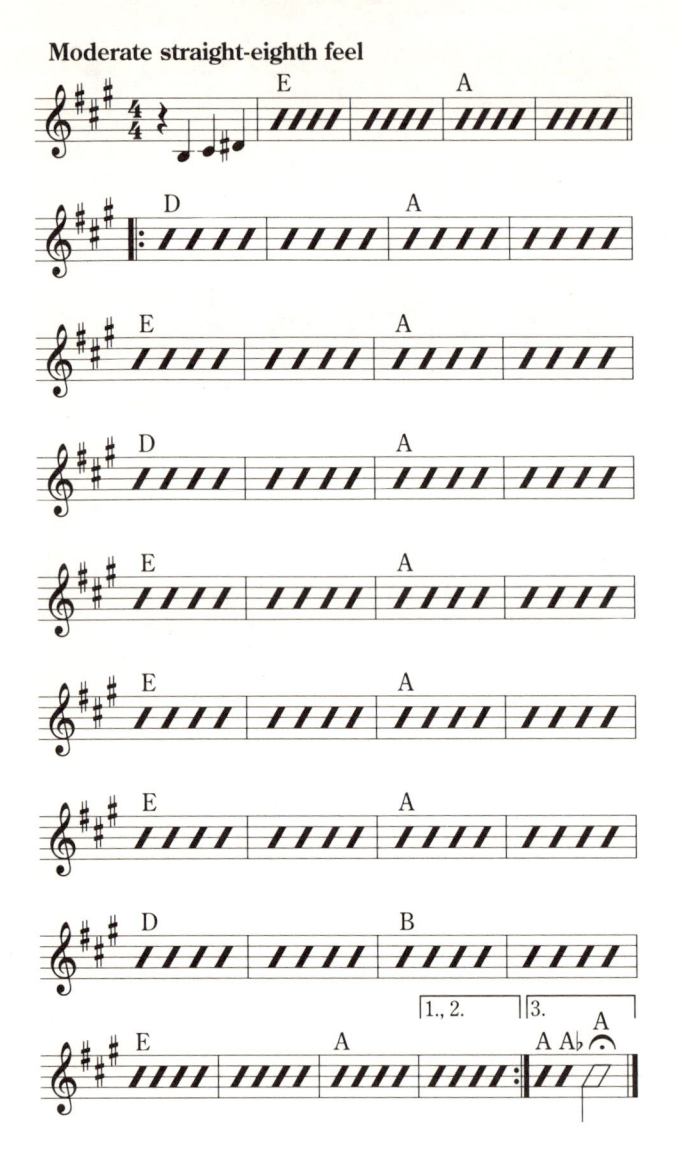

The Tricky Ricky Rag

Pattern 1: E Mixolydian scale with extension

Use this E Mixolydian scale for soloing over the E7 and A chords.

Pattern 2: D Mixolydian scale (two-octave)

This D Mixolydian scale will work well over the D7 and G chords.

Patterns 3 and 4: G riffs

Here are two sample riffs that should give you some ideas as to how to solo through the stoptime in measures 2 through 4.

pattern 3

pattern 4

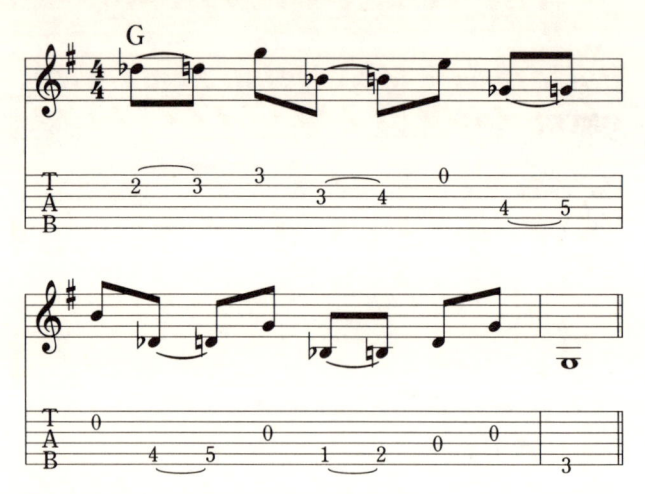

The Tricky Ricky Rag

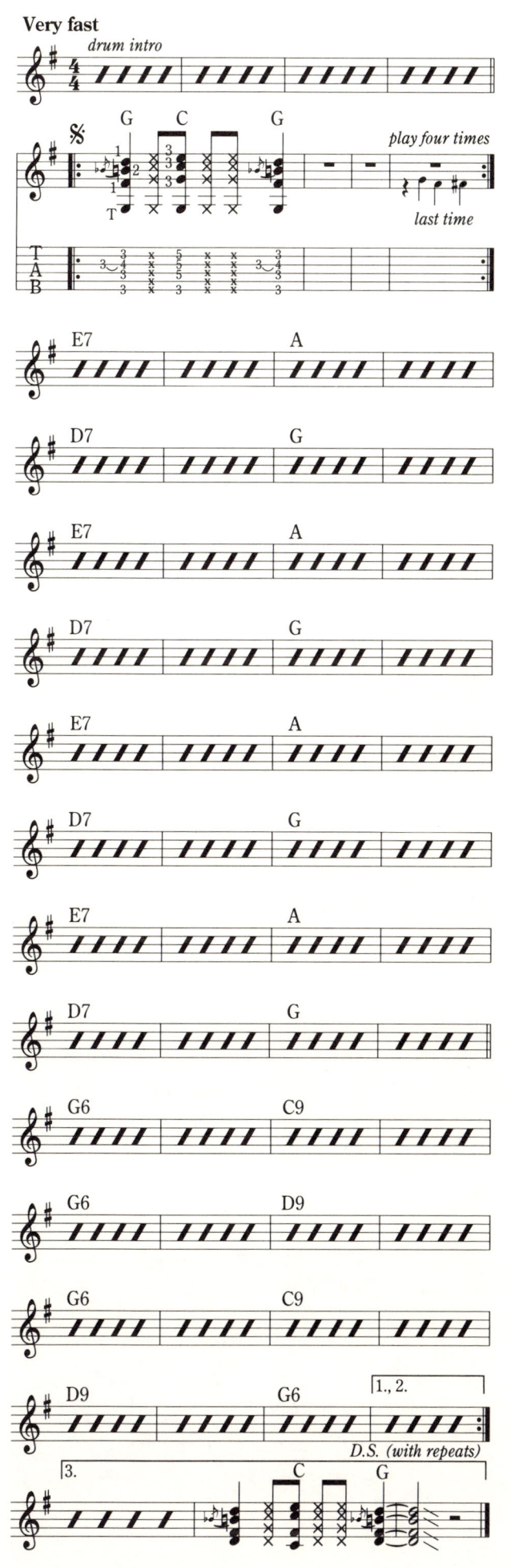

The Upbeat Cowboy

Pattern 1: A sample solo

Here is a whole flock of riffs joined together into a sample solo over the changes of the first eight bars of "The Upbeat Cowboy." The first two measures contain some typical pedal-steel guitar riffs on D and G chords. In measure 4 theres a descending pulloff riff on an A chord. Be sure to let the open E string ring as indicated. Measure 6 shows how you can put a touch of $D°7$ into a standard G lick when going to a D chord. (This standard jazz substitution works because of the strong similarity of $D°7$ to $G7♭9$.) The example finishes up with some arpeggios—notice the use of the G arpeggio against the A chord in the second half of measure 7.

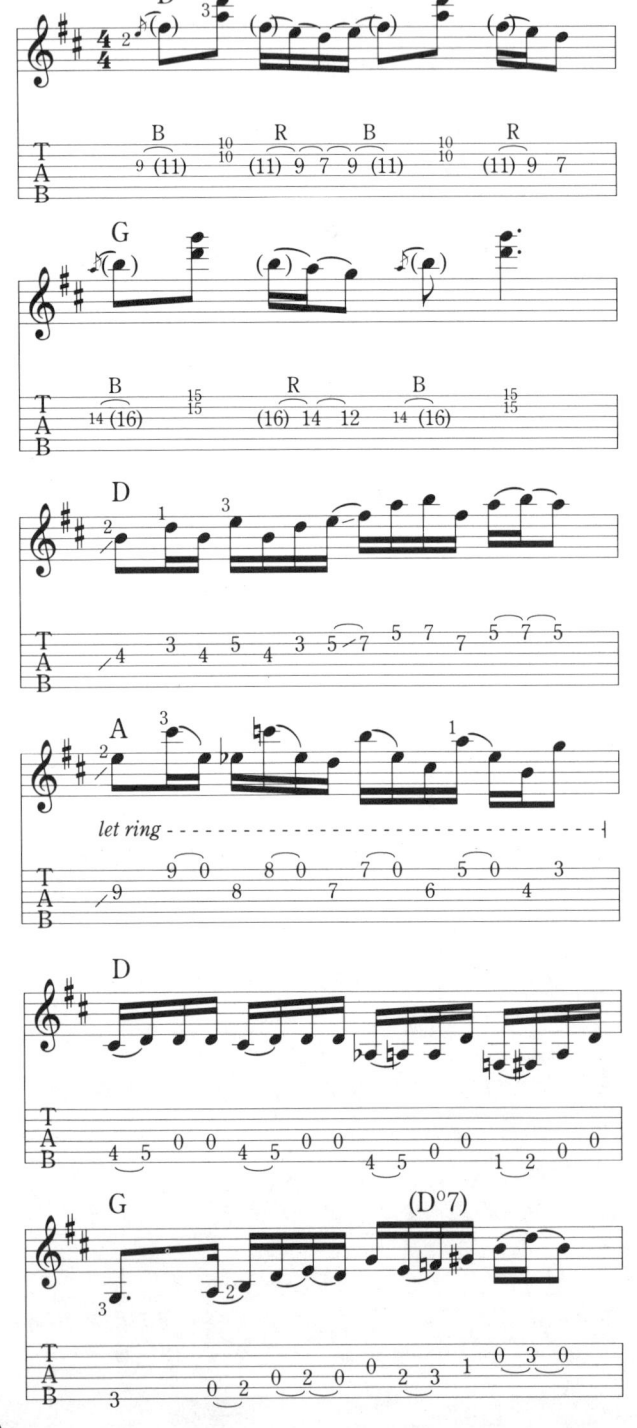

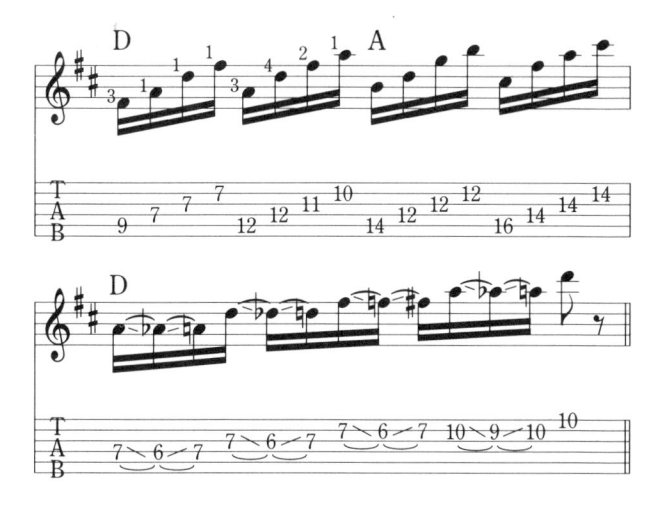

Pattern 2: Arpeggio riff with embellishments

This type of riff is a good one to play over measures 19 through 22. Notice that it also works over measures 23 through 26.

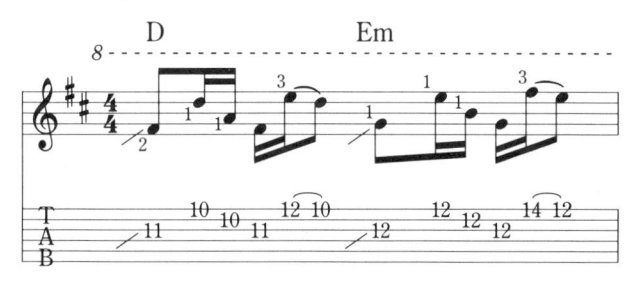

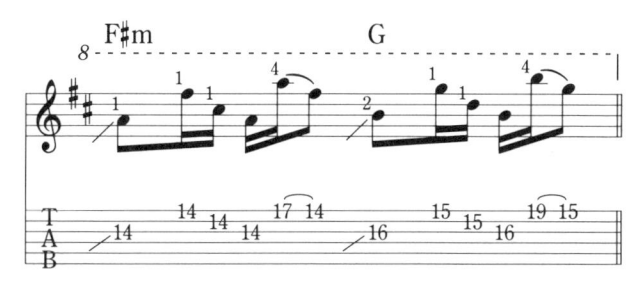

Pattern 3: A Mixolydian scale (two-octave)

Use this scale to solo over the A chords.

31

The Upbeat Cowboy

Moderate straight-eight feel